String Time Joggers
14 pieces for flexible ensemble
Kathy and David Blackwell

Contents

This symbol indicates the CD track numbers for each piece. The top number indicates the complete performance, and the bottom number the accompaniment alone. A tuning note (A) is located on track 29.

Cello

Sea Suite

1. Shark attack!

Printed in Great Britain

OXFORD UNIVERSITY PRESS, MUSIC DEPARTMENT, GREAT CLARENDON STREET, OXFORD OX2 6DP

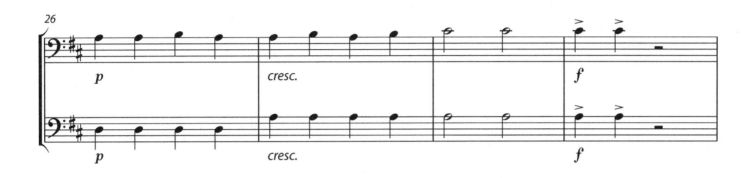

2. Barrier Reef

3. Cap'n Jack's Hornpipe

Lively ♩ = 84

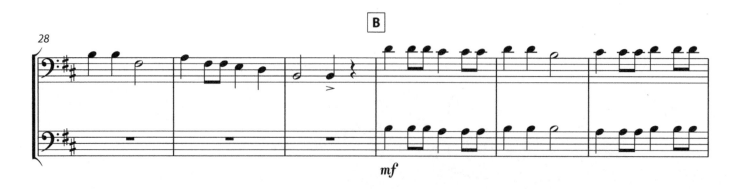

🎵 Jazz Suite

4. Simple syncopation

Happy ♩ = 112

5
○
19

5. Feelin' blue

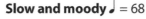

Slow and moody ♩ = 68

Fine

D.S. al Fine

9

6. Broadway or bust

Bright swing ♩ = 112

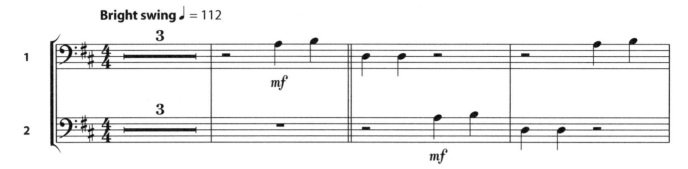

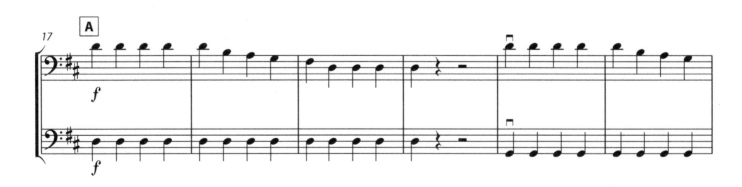

Jamaican Suite

7. Tinga Layo

(Part 1 and Harmony)

West Indian Trad.

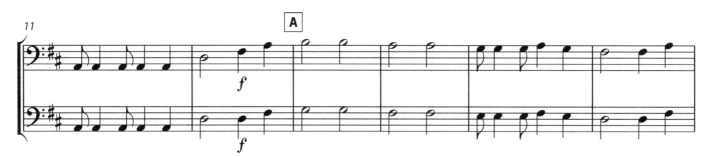

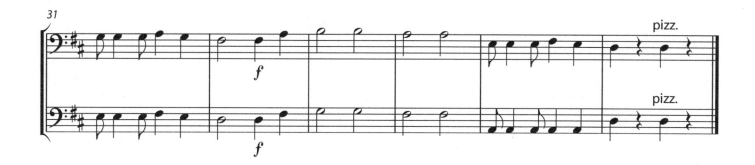

7. Tinga Layo
(Part 2)

West Indian Trad.

8. Jamaican lullaby

Jamaican Trad.

14

9. Kingston Calypso

Sunny ♩ = 130

Hollywood Suite

10. Spy movie 2

Menacing ♩ = 130

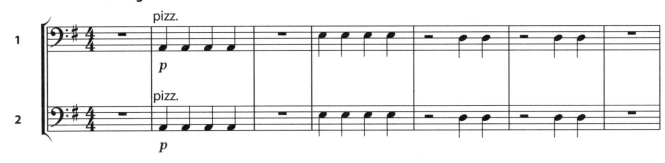

A

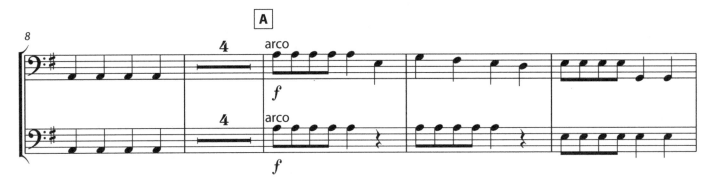

B

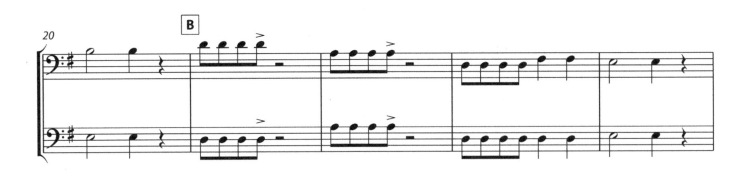

11. *Sad movie*

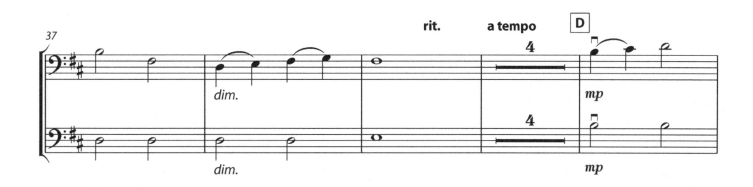

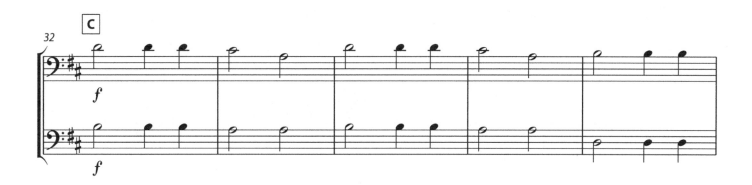

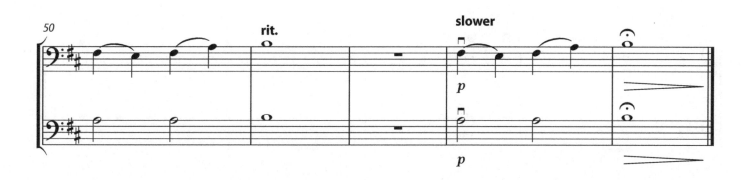

12. Action movie

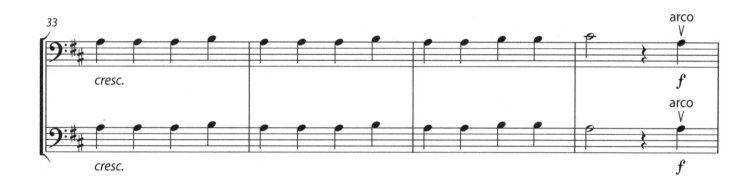

Extras

13. Cowboy song

14. Banuwa